Colours

Les couleurs

leh cool-*er*

Illustrated by Clare Beaton

Illustré par Clare Beaton

B SMALL PUBLISHING

BILINGUAL BOOKS

green

vert

vair

white

blanc

bloh

red

rouge

roo-jsh

black

noir

nwar

pink

rose

roz

blue

bleu

bl'

orange

orange

o-ronsh

grey

gris

gree

yellow

jaune

shown

brown

marron

mar-*roh*

purple

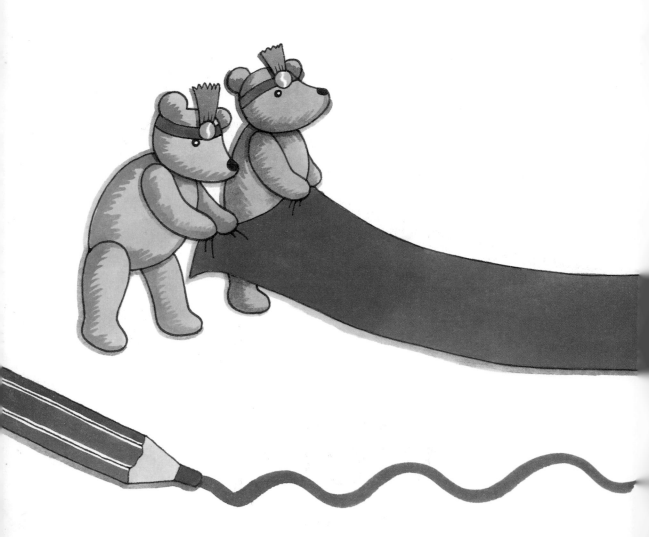

violet

vee-o-*leh*

A simple guide to pronouncing the French words

Les couleurs	leh cool-*er*	**Colours**
vert	vair	**green**
blanc	bloh	**white**
rouge	roo-jsh	**red**
noir	nwar	**black**
rose	roz	**pink**
bleu	bl'	**blue**
orange	o-*ronsh*	**orange**
gris	gree	**grey**
jaune	shown	**yellow**
marron	mar-*roh*	**brown**
violet	vee-o-*leh*	**violet**

Published by b small publishing
Pinewood, 3a Coombe Ridings, Kingston-upon-Thames, Surrey KT2 7JT
© b small publishing, 1993
1 2 3 4 5
All rights reserved.
No reproduction, copy or transmission of this publication may be made without written permission.
No part of this publication may be reproduced, stored in a retrieval system, or transmitted in any form or by any means,
electronic, mechanical, photocopying, recording or otherwise, without the prior permission of the publisher
Design: *Lone Morton*
Editorial: *Catherine Bruzzone*
Colour reproduction: Shiny Offset Printing Co. Ltd., Hong Kong.
Printed in Hong Kong by Wing King Tong Co Ltd.

ISBN 1 874735 10 7 (paperback)
ISBN 1 874735 15 8 (hardback)
British Library Cataloguing in Publication Data.
A catalogue record for this book is available from the British Library.